Fairy Tale Creatures

Giants

by Mark L. Lewis

FOCUS READERS

BEACON

www.focusreaders.com

Focus Readers is distributed by North Star Editions:
sales@northstareditions.com | 888-417-0195

Produced for Focus Readers by Red Line Editorial.

Photographs ©: Shutterstock Images, cover, 1, 4, 7, 8, 11, 13, 14–15, 16, 19, 21, 22, 25, 27, 29

Library of Congress Cataloging-in-Publication Data
Names: Lewis, Mark L., author.
Title: Giants : fairy tale creatures / Mark L. Lewis.
Description: Lake Elmo, MN : Focus Readers, [2022] | Series: Fairy tale creatures | Includes index. | Audience: Grades 2-3
Identifiers: LCCN 2021006327 (print) | LCCN 2021006328 (ebook) | ISBN 9781637390030 (hardcover) | ISBN 9781637390108 (paperback) | ISBN 9781637390177 (ebook) | ISBN 9781637390238 (pdf)
Subjects: LCSH: Giants--Juvenile literature.
Classification: LCC GR560 .L49 2022 (print) | LCC GR560 (ebook) | DDC 001.944--dc23
LC record available at https://lccn.loc.gov/2021006327
LC ebook record available at https://lccn.loc.gov/2021006328

Printed in the United States of America
Mankato, MN
082021

About the Author

Mark L. Lewis writes books for young readers in his spare time. He lives on a farm in Minnesota, where having a giant like Paul Bunyan would be very helpful.

Table of Contents

Chapter 1

In the Land of Giants

A giant wandered slowly through the forest. He was nearly as tall as the trees. The giant lifted his heavy ax. He chopped down a tree with just two swings. Its huge trunk crashed to the ground.

Stories say a giant's footprints can make craters or lakes.

The giant cut down several more trees. He tied the trunks together. Then he picked them all up. The giant carried them to a clearing. There, he started building a cabin.

The giant piled up logs to make the walls. Then he added a roof. By evening, the cabin was finished. The giant smiled and walked inside.

Fun Fact

One **legend** tells of a giant named Paul Bunyan. He had a pet ox named Babe.

Statues of Paul Bunyan and his ox stand in Bemidji, Minnesota.

Chapter 2

Ancient History

Myths of giants are thousands of years old. Some famous myths come from Greece and Norway. In **Norse** myths, giants were the parents of the gods. Over time, the giants and gods became enemies.

Many myths tell of giants fighting battles.

They fought against one another. Each wanted more power. But the gods were stronger. They took over.

People in Greece also told stories of gods fighting giants. The Greek gods fought a long war against the giants. The gods won. The giants were buried under the mountains.

Fun Fact

Norse myths say there will be more fighting between giants and gods. One day, this huge battle will end the world.

When the ground shook or volcanoes erupted, some people blamed giants.

They were trapped. But they were not dead. Some people believed these giants caused earthquakes. The giants were also said to make **volcanoes** shoot out fire.

Many other **cultures** have stories about giants. Some explain how the world was created. For example, Chinese myths tell of a giant named Pan Gu. He was born inside an egg. He split the egg's shell in two. One part became heaven. The other became the earth.

Fun Fact

The Greek god Zeus throws bolts of lightning. Myths say giants made the bolts.

A painting from a Mongolian temple shows Pan Gu (left) separating the land and sky.

In some versions of this myth, Pan Gu's body turned into the soil. His hair became plants. His eyes became the sun and moon. Other versions say he carved out the land and oceans.

STORY SPOTLIGHT

Giant's Causeway

People sometimes use legends of giants to explain parts of nature. One example comes from Northern Ireland. A legend tells of a giant named Finn McCool. He wanted to reach a nearby island. Another giant lived there. Finn built a bridge. He placed thousands of stones in the sea. They made a path toward the island.

The group of rocks really exists. It's known as the Giant's Causeway. Scientists think it was formed by **lava**. The lava oozed through cracks in the earth. When it reached the sea, it hardened into many **columns**.

The rocks of the Giant's Causeway stretch for nearly 4 miles (6.4 km).

Chapter 3

Large and Strong

Giants are known for their great size. In many stories, giants are more than 40 feet (12 m) tall. They tower over humans. And they are very strong. Some giants can pull trees up from the ground.

In some myths, giants' bodies are made of ice or stone.

Giants can also throw huge stones. Many are fierce fighters. Others are good at building. They can make mountains, islands, and rivers. Some stories tell of giants fishing for whales.

Some giants look similar to humans. Others are more like

Fun Fact

Stories say giants helped build Stonehenge. This ring of huge stones has stood in England for thousands of years.

Some of the huge rocks of Stonehenge are 30 feet (9.1 m) tall.

monsters. Norse myths describe several kinds of giants. There are frost giants, fire giants, and giants that live in the ocean. Some of them have multiple heads. Many have magical powers. For example, some can turn into animals such as wolves.

Many giants live in groups. The biggest giant is in charge. Other giants live in castles. They collect animals and **treasure**. Some try to trap people, too.

In Greek stories, some giants have only one eye. This type of giant is called a cyclops. It often

Fun Fact

In Greek myths, the gods live high above Earth. Once, giants stacked three mountains to try to reach them.

A cyclops is a one-eyed giant that eats people.

has a herd of sheep. Other Greek myths describe two-eyed giants. These giants fight against the gods.

Chapter 4

Smart or Not?

In Norse **mythology**, some giants were smart and brave. One giant could fight against an entire army of humans. Some giants even tried to **duel** the gods.

Giants can be fierce and stubborn. They can also be quick to start fights.

Other giants were not as smart. For example, one Norse myth tells of a giant named Hrungnir. He was huge and strong. He was also mean. His heart was made of stone. So was his head. As a result, he was not very smart.

In general, giants tend not to be very intelligent. People often trick them. In one story, a hero was trapped in a giant's castle. He challenged the giant to an eating contest. The hero hid a bag

A giant's castle is often filled with riches and treasure.

under his shirt. Instead of eating, he stuffed food into it. The trick worked. The giant ate so much he could not move. The hero escaped.

Some giants are dangerous. In North America, a Paiute legend describes giants with red hair. These giants attack people and eat them. Filipino myths also tell of a giant that eats people.

However, not all giants are evil. In Spain, stories say a giant owned

Fun Fact

A British legend tells of twin giants. Their names were Gog and Magog. These brave giants helped people.

In some legends, giants guard mountains or forests.

two castles. He was kind and took care of people. Another giant carved toys for children. People around the world continue to create new stories about giants.

FOCUS ON

Giants

Write your answers on a separate piece of paper.

1. Write a sentence that explains the main idea of Chapter 2.

2. Are you more interested in stories about kind giants or mean giants? Why?

3. How many eyes does a cyclops have?

A. one

B. two

C. six

4. Why might people use myths about giants to explain earthquakes?

A. Giants could use their size to fit in small places.

B. Giants could use their strength to shake the ground.

C. Giants could use their magic to disappear.

5. What does **intelligent** mean in this book?

*In general, giants tend not to be very **intelligent**. People often trick them.*

A. easy to run away from
B. easy to trick or fool
C. hard to trick or fool

6. What does **tower** mean in this book?

*In many stories, giants are more than 40 feet (12 m) tall. They **tower** over humans.*

A. to build with rocks
B. to be very short
C. to rise high above

Answer key on page 32.

Glossary

columns
Tall pieces of rock that stick up from the ground.

cultures
Groups of people and the ways they live, including their customs, beliefs, and laws.

duel
To fight or have a contest.

lava
Hot, melted rock that is released by a volcano onto Earth's surface.

legend
A well-known story from the past. Some legends are based on facts, but not all legends are true.

mythology
A culture's traditional stories that explain the world in some way.

Norse
Related to Norway or other parts of Scandinavia.

treasure
Something that is worth lots of money, such as gold or jewels.

volcanoes
Mountains or hills that can shoot out lava.

To Learn More

BOOKS

London, Martha. *Giants*. Minneapolis: Abdo Publishing, 2020.

Rowley, Kris Erickson. *Trolls*. Lake Elmo, MN: Focus Readers, 2019.

Sautter, A. J. *Discover Dragons, Giants, and Other Deadly Fantasy Monsters*. Mankato, MN: Capstone Press, 2018.

NOTE TO EDUCATORS

Visit **www.focusreaders.com** to find lesson plans, activities, links, and other resources related to this title.

Index

Answer Key: 1. Answers will vary; **2.** Answers will vary; **3.** A; **4.** B; **5.** C; **6.** C